AF228748

CHICAGO

294
94
Edison Park
Rogers park
West Ridge
Norwood Park
Forest Glen
Edge-water
North Park
Chicago O´Hare International Airport
190
90
Jefferson Park
Lincoln Square
Albany Park
Uptown
O'Hare
Portage Park
Irving Park
North Center
Lake View
Dunning
Avondale
294
Mont-clare
Belmont Cragin
Her-mosa
Logan Square
Lincoln Park
290
Austin
Humboldt Park
West Town
Near North Side
88
West Garfield Park
East Garfield Park
Near West Side
Chicago Loop
290
290
North Lawndale
90
Near South Side
Lower West Side
CHICAGO
South Lawndale
Armour Square
Douglas
LAKE MICHIGAN
55
McKinley Park
Bridge-port
Oak-land
Brighton Park
Grand Boulevard
Kenwood
Archer Heights
New City
Fuller Park
294
Garfield Ridge
West Elsdon
Gage Park
Washington Park
Hyde Park
94
55
Clearing
Woodlawn
West Lawn
Chicago Lawn
West Engle-wood
Engle-wood
Greater Grand Crossing
South Shore
Ashburn
Auburn Gresham
Avalon Park
South Chicago
Chatham
Burn-side
Calumet Heights
94
Washington Heights
Beverly
Pull-man
South Deering
East Side
90
Roseland
Mount Green-wood
94
Morgan Park
West Pullman
57
Riverdale
Hegewisch
294

CHICAGO

THE WINDY CITY

Jacqueline Hope Raynor

Firefly Books

A Firefly Book

Published by Firefly Books Ltd. 2025
Copyright © 2025 Firefly Books Ltd.
Text copyright © 2025 Jacqueline Hope Raynor
Photographs © as listed on page 94

All rights reserved. No part of this publication may be reproduced, stored in a retrieval system, or transmitted in any form or by any means, electronic, mechanical, photocopying, recording or otherwise, without the prior written permission of the Publisher.

First Printing

Library of Congress Control Number: 2025933807

Library and Archives Canada Cataloguing in Publication
Library and Archives Canada Cataloguing in Publication
Title: Chicago : the Windy City / Jacqueline Hope Raynor.
Names: Raynor, Jacqueline Hope, author.
Description: Includes index.
Identifiers: Canadiana 2025016583X | ISBN 9780228105664 (hardcover)
Subjects: LCSH: Chicago (Ill.)—Guidebooks. | LCSH: Chicago (Ill.)—
    Description and travel. | LCGFT: Guidebooks.
Classification: LCC F548.18 .R39 2025 | DDC 917.73/110444—dc23

Published in Canada by
Firefly Books Ltd.
50 Staples Avenue, Unit 1
Richmond Hill, Ontario
L4B 0A7

Published in the United States by
Firefly Books (U.S.) Inc.
P.O. Box 1338, Ellicott Station
Buffalo, New York
14205

Cover and interior design: Jacqueline Hope Raynor
Photo Editor: Cathy Hoshino

Printed in China | DC

INTRODUCTION

Chicago is a city of architectural gems, vibrant neighborhoods, beloved sports teams, prestigious cultural institutions and outstanding attractions. The major metropolis of the American heartland, Chicago boasts a population of nearly three million people, making it the third most populous city in the country.

Founded in 1833, Chicago was already famous for its stockyards, steel mills and railroads when the Great Chicago Fire of 1871 destroyed most of the city. But a great building boom followed the fire, and today the city's skyline is among the world's most famous and most beautiful.

Popularly called the Windy City because of its position on the southern shore of Lake Michigan, Chicago is also known as the City of Big Shoulders. Its generosity of spirit has welcomed waves of newcomers and travelers, and the city is justifiably proud of its reputation as a friendly town.

The city is composed of a patchwork of neighborhoods (77 at last count) and, not surprisingly, is a city of great food and regional specialties. It has a thriving downtown providing an almost unlimited variety of things to do and see. The contemporary Millennium Park offers music and the *Cloud Gate* sculpture lets visitors see their own reflection mirrored against the city's breathtaking skyline.

Chicago is a great sports town, too, where enthusiasts find professional teams of every major American sport. And there are renowned cultural institutions, a diverse and lively theater scene, the world-famous Navy Pier and other family attractions, the Magnificent Mile, and so much more.

But most of all, Chicago is a city of people. Some of them, including former President Barack Obama, are influential. All of them are extremely proud to be part of such a marvelous place.

From its soaring towers to its lakefront beaches, and from its diverse neighborhoods to its varied attractions, Chicago offers an abundance of things to see and do. We hope you'll enjoy them as you travel through the city in the pages of *Chicago: The Windy City.*

The Chicago "L" is the second-oldest rapid transit system in the United States (New York City has the oldest), and one of the few that offer 24-hour service. More than half of the 102.8 miles of transit line are elevated, which is why the system is called the "L," short for "elevated."

(Opposite) The Chicago Board of Trade dominates the end of LaSalle Street, which was named after early French explorer Sieur de La Salle. The 44-story Art Deco structure was so much taller than any other building that, when first constructed, it was believed that the sculpture of *Ceres* adorning its top was left faceless because no one in the surrounding buildings was high enough to see it. In fact, the sculptor intended the omission of the face to give the statue an ethereal and God-like look.

CHICAGO BOARD OF TRADE

The *Flamingo* sculpture in the Federal Plaza was created by Alexander Calder in 1973. The piece stands 53 feet tall and weighs more than 50 tons. It is the first artwork commissioned by the federal government as part of the Percentage Art Program under which a portion of the construction budget goes towards creating public art.

(Opposite) McCormick Tribune Ice Rink is a multi-purpose venue in the Loop area of Chicago. Opened in 2001, it acts as a free public outdoor ice skating rink for four months of the year and, as Park Grill Plaza, Chicago's largest outdoor dining facility for the rest of the year.

DRINK
PLAY
SHARE
PG
PARK GRILL
Millennium Park
PARK GRILL
McCormick Tribune Plaza

Opened in 2004, the futuristic Jay Pritzker Pavilion in Millennium Park was designed by Frank Gehry and hosts a diverse array of free cultural performances. The trellis of the Pavilion supports an aerial sound system which spans the 4,000 fixed seats and the 95,000-square-foot Great Lawn which can accommodate an additional 7,000 people. This state-of-the-art sound system, the first of its kind in the world, was designed to mimic the acoustics of an indoor concert hall by distributing enhanced sound equally over the whole area.

(Opposite) 875 North Michigan Avenue, formerly known as the John Hancock Center, is a 100-story skyscraper with a 360-degree observatory called TILT that is built to thrill. The first of its kind in the world, the TILT is an enclosed platform that literally tilts you out and over Michigan Avenue at a staggering 1,030 feet above the street.

In 1999 the Chicago Shakespeare Theater opened the doors of its multistory theater complex that can sit nearly 1,500 people. The company presents a wide range of plays, musicals and cultural events. It is one of the most prestigious theater companies in the Midwest.

(Opposite) The 3,300-foot Navy Pier juts into the lake from the base of Milton Lee Olive Park. Built in 1916, over the years the pier has served as a cargo facility, a summer playground and, during World War II, a training center for Navy pilots. It was rebuilt in the 1990s, and today Navy Pier is one of the city's premier attractions.

Located in the Streeterville neighborhood of Chicago, Navy Pier encompasses over 50 acres of shops, restaurants, live theaters, family attractions, parks, gardens and exhibition facilities. The Chicago Children's Museum (above) offers a unique interactive experience for kids, including the Art Studio, Playspace and Tinkering Lab.

(Opposite) Navy Pier's most visible attraction is the Centennial Wheel, a 200-foot-tall Ferris wheel that provides a thrilling ride and unbeatable views of the city's skyline and lakefront.

The Chicago Yacht Club "Race to Mackinac" is a 333-mile annual yacht race starting at the Chicago Harbor Lighthouse, just past Navy Pier, and ending at Mackinac Island. The "Mac" has run almost continuously since 1898 and is the oldest annual freshwater distance race in the world. Each year, over 300 boats and 3,000 sailors participate in teams that come from around the world.

Built in 1893, the Chicago Harbor Lighthouse is the only surviving lighthouse in Chicago. Today its crisp white conical tower rising between two red-roofed buildings is a familiar sight along Chicago's shoreline just east of Navy Pier, where the lighthouse continues to mark the harbor entrance. The Tall Ship *Windy* offers daily tours and private cruises around the harbor and lake.

The Civic Opera House, located in the Civic Opera Building (a 45-story office tower built in 1929), is one of the largest opera auditoriums in North America. It contains 3,276 seats and is the permanent home of the Lyric Opera of Chicago and the Joffrey Ballet.

(Opposite) Designed by internationally acclaimed artist Anish Kapoor and located in Millennium Park, *Cloud Gate* is one of the world's largest permanent outdoor art installations. Dedicated on May 15, 2006, it has become one of Chicago's most iconic sights. The sculpture, inspired by liquid mercury, was quickly nicknamed *The Bean* because of its shape.

JOHN G. SHEDD AQUARIUM
it's time to EXPLORE
Shedd
AQUARIUM
Exit only
EXIT ONLY
EXIT ONLY

The Shedd Aquarium opened in 1930 and is one of the largest aquariums in the United States. Thousands of ocean, lake and river creatures thrive within the marble octagon perched on the edge of Lake Michigan. A 90,000-gallon tank gives you a 360-degree tour of an underwater reef community, including sea turtles, sharks, stingrays, corals and sponges. Other permanent exhibits include Waters of the World, Amazon Rising and the Abbott Oceanarium.

The Fine Arts Building, originally constructed in 1885 by the Studebaker Brothers Manufacturing Company as a carriage sales and service operation, evolved into a haven for working artists. It includes lofts, art galleries, theater, dance and recording studios, interior and web design firms, and musical instrument makers.

(Opposite) The Griffin Museum of Science and Industry is one of the city's most popular attractions. The Museum boasts more than 2,000 exhibits, including a full-scale coal mine, a Pioneer Zephyr train and a U-505, the only German submarine in the United States.

Magdalene is an outdoor sculpture by Dessa Kirk located in Grant Park. In the springtime, tulips line the female figure's feet, and in the summertime the sculpture becomes part of the surrounding garden, as vines and flowers fill up the skirt of her dress.

(Opposite) Located on the northeastern tip of Northerly Island on Lake Michigan, the Adler Planetarium was the first planetarium in the United States. Founded in 1930 by local businessman Max Adler and declared a National Historic Landmark in 1937, the planetarium continues to evolve and boasts virtual reality programs, 3D theaters and a variety of internships, workshops and field trips.

The Field Museum of Natural History first opened in 1894 to display a collection of artifacts originally assembled for the 1893 Chicago World's Fair. Today, the exhibits explore more than 4.6 billion years of natural history, and human history from ancient Egypt to current world cultures. Known for its educational and scientific programs, the Museum maintains over 24 million specimens in its collection.

(Opposite) In May 2018 the Field Museum introduced their newest acquisition: *Máximo*, the titanosaur *Patagotitan mayorum*. This long-necked, plant-eating dinosaur lived over 100 million years ago, weighed about 70 tons, and is the largest dinosaur ever discovered. Cast from fossil bones excavated in Patagonia, Argentina, *Máximo* reaches 122 feet across Stanley Field Hall, stands 28 feet tall at the head and creates a sense of awe in the Museum's grand entranceway.

THE
MODERN
WING

This lion, one of a famous pair, stands guard at the Art Institute of Chicago, the oldest sections of which were built in 1893 as part of the Chicago World's Fair. The museum boasts treasures in every imaginable medium from the ancient world to the present day. The collection encompasses over 5,000 years of human history and contains more than 300,000 works.

(Opposite) The Modern Wing, as it's known, opened in 2009 and the 264,000-square-foot addition made the Art Institute of Chicago the second-largest art museum in the United States. It houses the museum's collections of 20th and 21st century art plus shops, classrooms, a cafe, a sculpture garden and a courtyard.

The *El Popocatepetl Tortilleria* mural by artists Brenda Lopez and
Manuel Macias, located in the Pilsen neighborhood of Chicago,
celebrates the area's Mexican heritage.

(Opposite) Founded in 2000, The National Museum of Puerto Rican
Arts and Culture is housed in the historic Humboldt Park Receptory
Building and Stables within Humboldt Park, a 207-acre park on the
West Side of Chicago. It hosts visual arts exhibitions, community
education events and festivals, and is dedicated to showcasing
Puerto Rican arts and cultural exhibitions year-round.

Old and new meet seamlessly in downtown Chicago. Installed in 1897, this beautiful art deco bronze clock hangs 17 feet above the sidewalk. More than 100 years later and just a few yards away, Blues legend Muddy Waters was honored in this colorful, nine-story mural created by Brazilian street artist Eduardo Kobra.

(Opposite) Located on the Magnificent Mile, the Wrigley Building was built in the early 1920s to house the corporate headquarters of the Wrigley Company. It was Chicago's first air-conditioned office building. Clad in glazed terra-cotta, the entire building is occasionally hand-washed to preserve its gleaming white façade.

One of Chicago's defining features is its location on Lake Michigan, which includes 26 miles of stunning shoreline. Much of the waterfront is connected by the Lakefront Trail, a scenic pedestrian pathway stretching for more than 18 miles and offering stunning views of the lake and city skyline. The trail, popular in all seasons with walkers, bikers and runners, connects many of the city's lakefront parks, beaches, museums, neighborhoods and waterfront restaurants. Even the visiting Canada Geese love it!

The Chicago Jazz Festival and the Chicago Blues Festival have been hugely popular events for over 40 years, taking place at and around Petrillo Music Shell in Grant Park. In 2017, due to the badly aging venue, both events moved to Millennium Park and are now part of the city's free summer music festival lineup. The festivals showcase Chicago's local talent alongside national and international artists and raise awareness and appreciation for some of the city's most beloved music.

(Opposite) With its monolithic façade, the House of Blues is one of the premier music venues in the city.

(Following) Buckingham Fountain, the Baroque centerpiece of Grant Park, is modeled after the Latona Fountain at Palace of Versailles outside Paris, but is twice its size. The fountain spurts water 150 feet into the air throughout the day, from May through October.

HOUSE OF BLUES
What'll You Have?
What'll You Have?
BIN
36

Oak Street Beach is located on Lake Shore Drive near the Gold Coast and Streeterville neighborhoods. This popular summer hotspot offers chair, bike and volleyball rentals along with a spectacular view of the city skyline and Lake Michigan. Throughout the summer the beach hosts popular amateur and professional volleyball tournaments. In the winter, the Polar Plunge brings brave Chicagoans together to raise money for local charities.

Since opening its doors in 1870, the Palmer House hotel has been a Chicago landmark. Rebuilt and renovated twice, it was bought by Conrad Hilton in 1945 and renamed The Palmer House Hilton. It's many famous visitors include American presidents, writers Mark Twain, Charles Dickens and Oscar Wilde, and entertainers Frank Sinatra, Louis Armstrong, Lena Horne and Ella Fitzgerald.

(Opposite) Michigan Avenue is the home of some of the city's top attractions including the Art Institute of Chicago, Millennium Park and the Magnificent Mile with its exclusive stores, restaurants and hotels. The Water Tower, located along the "Mag Mile," survived the Great Chicago Fire and now serves as a Chicago Office of Tourism gallery.

This 12-foot-tall bronze statue of Hall
of Fame basketball legend Michael
Jordan, known as *The Spirit*, stands
inside the atrium of the United Center.
The Center is the largest arena by total
area in the nation and home to the
Chicago Bulls (NBA) and the Chicago
Blackhawks (NHL).

(Opposite) Wrigley Field, the oldest
National League ballpark, has served
as the home of the Chicago Cubs (MLB)
since 1916. Nicknamed the "Friendly
Confines," Wrigley can be either
friendly or unfriendly to the pitchers; it
all depends on the way the wind blows.

Walter Payton is honored with a statue at the entrance to the stadium. A running back who played for 13 seasons with the Chicago Bears, he was nicknamed "Sweetness" and is widely regarded as one of the greatest football players of all time.

(Opposite) Soldier Field, a multipurpose stadium on the Near South Side of Chicago, opened in 1924 and underwent an extensive renovation in 2003. The stadium is home to the Chicago Bears (NFL) and Chicago Fire FC (MLS). It also regularly hosts stadium concerts and other large-crowd events. In 1968, it hosted the inaugural World Games of the Special Olympics, as well as the second World Games in 1970. Other historic events held here have included large rallies with speeches by Amelia Earhart, Franklin D. Roosevelt and Martin Luther King Jr.

St. Patrick's Day is a popular event in Chicago. In time for various parades throughout the city, boats spread nontoxic dye through the water until the river turns completely green. It's hard to forget the celebrations since the color lasts for days.

(Opposite) *The Bowman* is one of Croatian sculptor Ivan Meštrović's two mounted warriors at the Congress Plaza entrance to Grant Park. The sculptures were made in Zagreb and installed in the park in 1928; each statue stands 17 feet high and rests atop an 18-foot granite pedestal. Curiously, *The Bowman* does not have a bow (and *The Spearman* does not have a spear). Several myths have grown up around the "missing" weapons but, in fact, there never were weapons — the artist preferred to leave their actual shape to the viewer's imagination.

First opened in 1921, the legendary Chicago Theatre is considered the first lavish movie palace in the country. It has evolved to serve a variety of entertainment needs, from musical acts to stand-up comedy. The building and its famous illuminated signs have become one of the most recognizable sites on State Street.

(Opposite) Standing 50 feet tall and weighing over 160 tons, the untitled statue nicknamed the *Chicago Picasso* in Daley Plaza sparked controversy when it was first unveiled in 1967. Picasso gifted the piece to the city, refusing to accept the $100,000 offered to him. He gave no explanation for what the sculpture was meant to be but, in a later interview, he claimed it represented the head of his Afghan hound, Kabul.

The Chicago Cultural Center is home to the world's largest Tiffany stained-glass dome. Completed in 1897, the dome is composed of 1,134 square feet of colorful mosaics, including 30,000 individual panes of glass. Every year, thousands of visitors come to stare up at the breathtaking masterpiece.

The Beaux Arts-style Great Hall at Union Station is remarkable for its Corinthian columns, five-story barrel-vaulted atrium ceiling and marble floor. The station opened in 1925 and, during World War II, it handled as many as 100,000 people daily.

Completed in 1888, the Rookery Building is an architectural
gem in the center of Chicago's downtown financial district.
Entering through the imposing Romanesque exterior, visitors
are delighted by the light and airy interior made possible
by the innovative use of iron framing. The interior lobby
(opposite) was remodeled by Frank Lloyd Wright in 1905.

River cruises provide a unique perspective for appreciating Chicago's soaring towers and other architecturally significant sites.

(Opposite) The On Leong Merchants Association Building in Chicago's Chinatown opened in 1928, the first building to display the neighborhood's strong cultural background. The Merchants Association used it as an immigrant assistance center and it was informally referred to as Chinatown's "city hall." In 1993 it was designated a Chicago landmark, renovated and renamed the Pui Tak Center.

Opened in 2003, the McCormick Tribune Campus Center was designed by noted architect Rem Koolhaas as an addition to the main campus of the Illinois Institute of Technology, located in the Bronzeville neighborhood of Chicago. A major design challenge was posed by the noise of the Green Line tracks passing over the lot. The solution was to enclose a 530-foot section of the tracks in a stainless-steel tube, thus insulating and minimizing the vibration passing between the two structures.

Beginning in May 1892, Chicago's Polonia — the largest Polish community outside of Warsaw — proudly participate in the Polish Constitution Day Parade. Each summer, the annual Taste of Polonia Festival in Jefferson Park attracts over 35,000 people and has grown to be the largest Polish festival in the country. Polish is the fourth most widely spoken language in Chicago behind English, Spanish and Mandarin.

DuSable Bridge's two double-deck leaves carry Michigan Avenue and a lower-level road over the river; there are two levels of vehicular and pedestrian traffic. Each leaf weighs 3,400 tons but, due to the fine balance of the counterweights, two 108-horsepower motors are all that is needed to open and close the bridge.

(Opposite) There are 37 movable bridges along the Chicago and Calumet rivers and, throughout the boating season, the downtown bridges are lifted to allow high-masted sailboats access to and from the lake.

The Willis Tower (opposite), still locally known as the Sears Tower, is a 1,451-foot skyscraper in the Loop area of Chicago. It's distinctive black façade, made of black aluminum and bronze-tinted glass, is an iconic part of Chicago's skyline. Each year, more than 1.7 million people visit the all-glass Skydeck observation center on the 103rd floor to experience breathtaking views of the city.

An elaborate gate with the sculpted head of a bull is all that remains of the once famous Union Stock Yards that operated in Chicago for over one hundred years before closing in 1971. From the Civil War until the 1920s more meat was processed here than anywhere else in the world. The Chicago firefighters memorial, *The Fallen 21*, can be seen in the background.

(Opposite) Located in the heart of downtown Chicago, Monroe Harbor is home to the Chicago Yacht Club and Columbia Yacht Club. With 10 boat harbors located within parks along the lakefront, the Chicago Park District also operates the nation's largest municipal harbor system.

A statue of Swedish biologist Carl Linnaeus welcomes visitors to the Midway Plaisance park of the University of Chicago.

(Opposite) The William Rainey Harper Memorial Library at the University of Chicago, a Gothic-style building that is considered an iconic campus landmark, was inspired by the world-renowned architecture of Cambridge and Oxford universities in England. When it opened in June 1912 the building featured state-of-the-art technology: telephones and a system of pneumatic tubes were installed to transmit book orders. It served as the University's main circulation library for 60 years and was then renovated to serve as a study center.

The restored Jane Addams Hull-House, located on the University of Illinois Chicago campus, was bought by its namesake in 1889 to serve as a base for her settlement house movement that aided new immigrants to America.

(Opposite) The Rockefeller Memorial Chapel, funded by oil magnate John D. Rockefeller, was dedicated in 1928. Designed by Bertram Goodhue in English Gothic style, the enormous limestone chapel features some of the largest stained-glass windows in the United States.

Like a number of other churches built in the Polish Cathedral style, the opulent Mary of the Angels church, located in Chicago's Bucktown neighborhood, was modeled on St. Peter's Basilica in Rome. It is considered one of the finest specimens of Roman Renaissance architecture in the United States.

(Opposite) Holy Name Cathedral is in one of the largest Roman Catholic dioceses in the United States. Dedicated in 1875, the cathedral contains many beautiful examples of the Gothic revival architectural style. From the massive bronze doors that weigh 1,200 pounds each, to the majestic organ constructed by Flentrop Orgelbouw of Zaandam, Netherlands, the cathedral is truly awe-inspiring.

The Chicago Marathon, officially known as the Bank of America Chicago Marathon, was first held in 1977. Beginning and ending in Grant Park it is one of the fastest-growing road races in the world, due in part to its largely flat course. Approximately 50,000 runners participate each year.

(Opposite) Opened in 1930 and built in the same Art Deco style as the Chicago Board of Trade Building, the Merchandise Mart was the largest building in the world in terms of floorspace (4 million square feet) until it was surpassed by the Pentagon in 1943. The Mart had its own ZIP code and its own station on the "L."

Garfield Park Conservatory, still one of the largest conservatories in the United States, was constructed in 1907 and was fondly referred to as "landscape art under glass." The conservatory underwent a major restoration project in the 1990s. Contemporary works like *Les Trois Graces* by Niki de Saint Phalle have been displayed in the conservatory and brought it joyfully into the 21st century. The artwork displayed continues to evolve and attracts thousands of Chicagoans and visitors from all over the world.

Osaka Japanese Garden in Jackson Park provides an oasis of calm in the busy city.
Jackson Park has been selected by the Obama Foundation as the site of the future
Obama Presidential Center.

The Aqua Tower, completed in 2009, is a unique addition to the Chicago skyline. The 87-story mixed-use building is topped by a terrace with gardens, gazebos, pools, a running track and a fire pit. Inspired by the topography of the Great Lakes region, the curved balconies give the building a deceptively soft look and protect it from harsh winds — one of the most difficult challenges in skyscraper engineering.

The Marina Towers, two mixed-
use high-rise towers opened in
1963, are part of the Marina City
complex, which also includes a hotel,
auditorium and marina. Quickly
nicknamed the "corncob towers,"
they were the tallest reinforced
concrete buildings in the world
when completed.

Jean Baptiste Point DuSable, a pioneer trader of Haitian descent, is regarded as the first permanent non-Native settler in the area that later became Chicago, arriving there sometime in the 1780s. He is recognized as the city's founder. A school, museum, harbor, park, bridge and road are among some of the things named in his honor.

(Opposite) Considered one of the most desirable neighborhoods in Chicago, Lincoln Park contains a beautiful park, historic tree-lined streets and an eclectic mix of houses and apartment buildings.

The *Agora* sculptures are a group of 106 headless, nine-foot-tall cast iron figures in Grant Park. The sculptures were created by Polish artist Magdalena Abakanowicz and installed in 2006. The name *Agora* comes from the Greek word for "meeting place."

(Opposite) Surrounded by downtown skyscrapers, the BP Pedestrian Bridge connects Millennium Park and Maggie Daley Park, creating an unexpectedly peaceful spot in the middle of the city. The Chicago Park District oversees more than 600 parks containing over 8,800 acres of municipal parkland, including field houses, beaches, pools, museums, world-class botanical conservatories, lagoons and bird and wildlife gardens, all within the city limits.

The Nathan G. Moore House is one of the most famous of Frank Lloyd Wright's early designs. Completed in 1895 in the Tudor Style, the structure was seriously damaged by fire in 1922, at which point Wright undertook its adaptation and restoration.

The home that Frank Lloyd Wright designed for Frederick C. Robie in 1908 has become one of the most famous structures of the 20th century. It expresses Wright's influential Frairie Style, marked by long, horizontal lines, dramatic overhangs and art glass windows.

The Greek Revival Clarke-Ford House in the Prairie Avenue Historic District was built for a wealthy hardware dealer in 1836 and is considered the city's oldest structure.

(Opposite) The Ernest Hemingway Birthplace Museum is where the author was born on July 21, 1899. The Queen Anne house has been completely restored and is furnished as it would have been at the turn of the 20th century.

The *Standing Lincoln* statue, also known as *Abraham Lincoln: The Man*, is a 12-foot bronze statue by Augustus Saint-Gaudens. It is widely thought to be one of the greatest masterpieces of public art from the 19th century. It portrays Lincoln in a natural posture with rumpled clothes, rather than as a deity as previous statues had done.

(Opposite) Lincoln Park, Chicago's largest park, receives over 20 million visitors each year, second only to Central Park in New York City. The park contains the Lincoln Park Zoo, Lincoln Park Conservatory, an outdoor theater, a rowing canal, the Chicago History Museum, the Peggy Notebaert Nature Museum, the Alfred Caldwell Lily Pool, the North Pond Nature Sanctuary and the North Avenue Beach. Its wealth of resources enriches the lives of many Chicagoans.

The section of South Michigan Avenue across from Millennium Park is one of the world's most-recognized streets. The 12-block stretch of historic buildings (some dating back to the 1880s) is an outdoor museum displaying the work of the city's best architects. This "streetwall" was designated a Chicago Landmark in 2002, and the façades of the buildings cannot be changed without city approval. Crown Fountain in the foreground shows the faces of hundreds of people displayed on a giant rotating video screen. (Above) Every few minutes, water shoots out of the mouth of one of the people pictured.

(Following) One of Chicago's most popular spots, North Avenue Beach in Lincoln Park has plenty of room for sunbathing and relaxing, as well as trails for running, cycling, skateboarding and rollerblading.

PHOTO CREDITS

ALAMY

Rainer Lesniewski: 2; Todd Bannor: 17; Imago: 23; Gina Rodgers: 27; robertharding: 30; UrbanImages: 34; D Guest Smith: 35; Jon Lovette: 38; Image of sport: 46; B. Leighty/Photri Images: 60; Eric Nathan: 65; Chon Kit Leong: 67; Roy Johnson: 68; Pat A. Robinson/ZUMA Press Wire: 74; Steve Skjold: 76; Serhii Chrucky: 80; Todd Bannor: 86; CNMages: 87; Eric Nathan: 89; Travellaggio: 92–93; Bruce Leighty: 96

iSTOCK

roman_slavik: 6–7; Uncle-Ulee: 14; halbergman: 63

SHUTTERSTOCK

EarthScape ImageGraphy: 8; Andriy Blokhin: 9; James Kirkikis: 10; Miune: 11; Felix Mizioznikov: 12; Matthew Dicker: 13; Kobby Dagan: 15; wonderlustpicstravel: 16; Thomas Barrat: 18; Dennis MacDonald: 19; Atosan: 20; Edlane De Mattos: 21; Joseph Hendrickson: 22; Thomas Barrat: 24; LoRo: 25; 4kclips: 26; Sergii Figurnyi: 28; Jon Rehg: 29; adolf martinez soler: 31; Eddie J. Rodriquez: 32; Henryk Sadura: 33; T-I: 36; GagliardiPhotography: 37; MattL_Images: 39; Lucky-photographer: 40–41; ChicagoPhotographer: 42; pics721: 43; Nagel Photography: 44; EQRoy: 45; ChicagoPhotographer: 47; seanccochran: 48: Joseph Hendrickson: 49; Moab Republic: 50; Aaron of L.A. Photography: 51; Nicola Patterson: 52–53; Felix Lipov: 54; stellamc: 55; Thomas Barrat: 56; wonderlustpicstravel: 57; Krikof971: 58; Kenneth Sponsler: 59; Roberto Galan: 61; Cal F: 62; James Kirkikis: 64; ChicagoPhotographer: 66; elesi: 69; ChicagoPhotographer: 70; Flashon Studio: 71; Edlane De Mattos: 72; Carlos Yudica: 73; Jillian Cain Photography: 75; Wirestock Creators: 77; gdvcom: 78; alekseigl: 79; blvdone: 81; Gianfranco Vivi: 82; Nicola Patterson: 83; Sandra Foyt: 84; Pamela Brick: 85; Oren Ravid: 88; ALEXANDRE F FAGUNDES: 90; fukez84: 91

This statue of a saxophone player stands at the intersection of Martin Luther King Drive and 47th Street in the Bronzeville neighborhood.